1800~1850 Americans Move Westward

Written by NAUNERLE FARR

Edited by D'ANN CALHOUN

Illustrated by FRANK REDONDO

Editorial consultant LAWRENCE W. BLOCH

A VINCENT FAGO PRODUCTION

Pendulum Press, Inc.
West Haven, Connecticut

ISBN 0-88301-227-8

Published by
PENDULUM PRESS, INC.
An Academic Industries, Inc., Company
The Academic Building
Saw Mill Road
West Haven, Connecticut 06516

Printed in the United States of America

To the Teacher:

With educators everywhere concerned about the literacy of the nation's children, attention has been focused primarily on the reading curriculum. Reading teachers can select from literally thousands of varied programs for their classes. Yet social studies teachers, faced with an equal amount of material to cover, are often at a loss. Although many history texts are available, they all seem to offer information alone at the expense of motivation. Out of this understanding the **Basic Illustrated History of America** series was developed.

Motivation is the basic premise and the outstanding strength of these texts. Each book was written in the belief that children will learn and remember whatever they find enjoyable. Through illustration, they are drawn into the reading matter, and learning begins.

Besides motivating, the illustrations provide clues to the meanings of words. Unfamiliar vocabulary is defined in footnotes. Every volume in the series has been edited to simplify the reading. And, since the interest level extends as far as the adult reader, students in all grades—even in remedial classes—will enjoy these texts. Finally, companion student activity books guide the reading with vocabulary drills and exercises on comprehension.

The **Basic Illustrated History of America** series, then, offers a new concept in the teaching of American history, yet one which does not subordinate content to form. Meticulously researched historical data provides the authenticity for costumes and architecture in each era. Together, the features of this unique series will make learning an enjoyable experience for the student—and a rewarding one for the teacher.

The editors

contents

Thomas Jefferson, president of the United States in 1802, received important news.

We are sure of it, Mr. President. The story is true.

France has taken over New Orleans and the Louisiana Territory from Spain!

And all our western settlers must send their goods through New Orleans.

Whoever owns that port is our enemy!

We can hardly fight France if she decides to close it!

There might be another way! I will write to Robert Livingston. And I will send James Monroe to France to help Livingston.

In Paris a few weeks later, Robert Livingston, minister to France, received a letter.

President Jefferson asks me to offer to buy New Orleans from the French! I must speak to Tallyrand* very carefully.

* famous French foreign minister

A special messenger brought an order to James Monroe.

This paper makes me Envoy Extraordinary and Minister Plenipotentiary** to both France and Spain.

What a grand title!

That is to flatter the French, and to impress them with my authority.

** a special ambassador

This was the news that greeted Monroe when he arrived in Paris two days later.

Napoleon offers to sell us the whole of that great territory? And most of it still not explored! Why would he do that?

He is on the edge of another war with England . . .

I see, I see! With the strong English navy between France and Louisiana, he stands to lose it anyway.

So he might as well sell it and get something out of it! Exactly!

We were not told to buy so much—or to spend so much.

But we would more than double our size! We would remove the rule of all other countries from the Mississippi valley! It is the chance of a lifetime!

Talks took place with Tallyrand. They agreed on a price of fifteen million dollars—about four cents an acre. This was the biggest real estate deal in history!

The Louisiana Purchase Territory 1803

In New Orleans on December 20, 1803, the French flag was taken down. The American flag was raised. Now the Louisiana Territory belonged to the United States!

Thomas Jefferson was very curious about the western lands. He had always wanted to know more about them. Now they were part of the United States, and they were still unknown to most Americans.

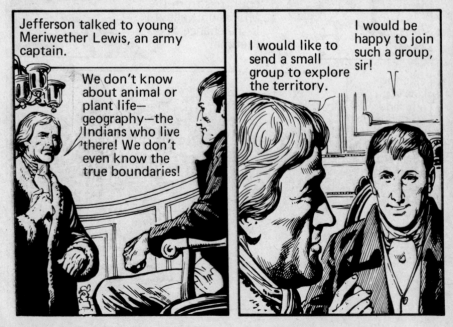

Jefferson talked to young Meriwether Lewis, an army captain.

We don't know about animal or plant life—geography—the Indians who live there! We don't even know the true boundaries!

I would like to send a small group to explore the territory.

I would be happy to join such a group, sir!

You are my choice to head the group, Meriwether.

I would be glad to do so, sir. Could I have William Clark as a partner?

He is a younger brother of George Rogers Clark, and he knows frontier life very well!

He is a good choice. Pick your own men.

At Jefferson's request, Congress voted $2,500 for the expenses of the group. Lewis made the preparations. They set up headquarters at St. Louis. In the spring of 1804, they were ready to move up the Missouri River on the first stage of their trip across the unknown lands. They had a keelboat, two lighter boats and tons of supplies.

The Missouri had a swift current, sandbars, snags, whirlpools, collapsing banks. Sometimes they went thirty miles in a day; often, only five or six.

Besides twenty-eight soldiers and several boatmen, there was Clark's black servant, York, and Lewis's dog, Scammon.

The river provided all sorts of fish, including the biggest catfish they had ever seen.

We'll only report things as true that we've seen for ourselves.

One hundred twenty-six pounds! I've heard of 200-pounders!

They made notes of everything, this being one of the purposes of the trip. They were surprised at the many birds they saw.

The pelicans are comical!

A cormorant!

There are hundreds of whooping cranes!

These rare birds were once common in the midwestern states.

Another important job was to note the different kinds of Indians they met. They were to make friends with them if they could, for these Indians were now part of the United States.

On May 22, they traded for fresh meat with a hunting party of friendly Kickapoos.

You give us four deer . . .

We give you two bottles of whiskey.

Good! Good!

Later their own hunters began to bring in food.

There is much game. We have seen black bear, deer, elk . . .

And off to the west we could see buffalo herds— thousands of buffalo!

On June 12 they met a raft headed south, loaded with furs and Frenchmen.

'Allo, Americains! Bonjour, M'sieus*!

Hello, the raft! Greetings, Frenchmen!

The two boats tied up for a visit. The captains wanted to learn everything possible about the trip ahead.

What about the Indians upriver?

High up you'll find the Mandans. They are good Indians. But before the Mandans you'll be in Sioux country!

And the Sioux?

The Sioux are sly and mean. They will ask for gifts.

And there are thousands of them! You won't get through Sioux country without trouble.

* Hello, Americans! Good day, sirs!

As the Frenchmen had told them, upriver the Sioux Indians lined the banks.

We must arrange a powwow* with them. That's part of our job.

It's true—there must be thousands!

Lewis and Clark went ashore with a small guard.

They were taken to the Indian camp, and Lewis made a speech.

We have come from the great white chief of America. Your old fathers the French and Spanish have gone . . .

* conference with Indians

We bring you American flags and medals. The American father wants his children to live in peace together . . .

They gave gifts to the Indians.

Then one of the chiefs stepped forward.

You insult us with cheap gifts! You must give much more— tobacco and whiskey! But no matter how much, you will not be allowed to go upriver!

The Sioux have many warriors— as many as the leaves on the trees!

If white men go upriver, you will be followed and killed! All, all of you!

The moment was tense. Clark drew his sword; the guards raised their rifles.

We're Americans! This is our nation! We'll share it with you in peace and friendship. But if you try to fight us, we'll wipe you off the earth!

Lewis and Clark returned safely to their boat. There they talked.

If we let them have their way, if we show any weakness, they'll attack.

And if we are forced to fight, they will also attack!

We can defend ourselves and leave safely. But an attack means war with the Sioux and the end of our trip!

First the Sioux chiefs said they would fight. Then they begged for peace. They came aboard, left again, and tried to keep the boats from moving. The group was always on guard. When the boats moved, the Indians followed along the banks for four days. But at last they went away.

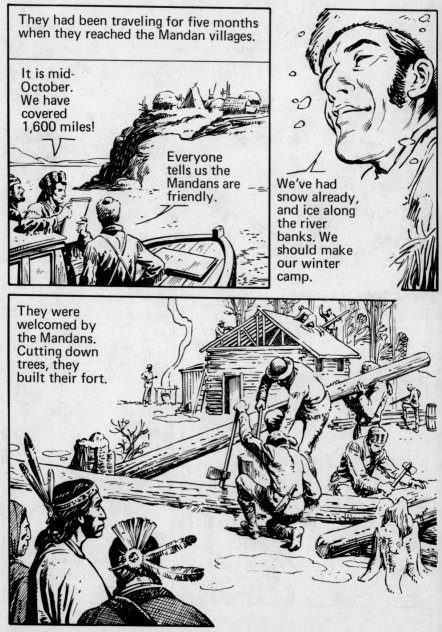

They had been traveling for five months when they reached the Mandan villages.

It is mid-October. We have covered 1,600 miles!

Everyone tells us the Mandans are friendly.

We've had snow already, and ice along the river banks. We should make our winter camp.

They were welcomed by the Mandans. Cutting down trees, they built their fort.

At times the temperature was fifty degrees below zero. When the weather was good, they worked on canoes.

On March 3 there was a welcome sight.

As the river narrows and becomes more shallow, we'll use these canoes.

Look! Ducks going north!

Spring is on its way!

Charbonneau, a French trapper, was in the Mandan village. He talked to Lewis.

My wife is an Indian— a Shoshone from west of the mountains.

Yes?

She was captured when she was a child. But she remembers the Shoshone language and some of the country. If she went with you, this might be helpful.

Indeed, yes! No one else knows that language!

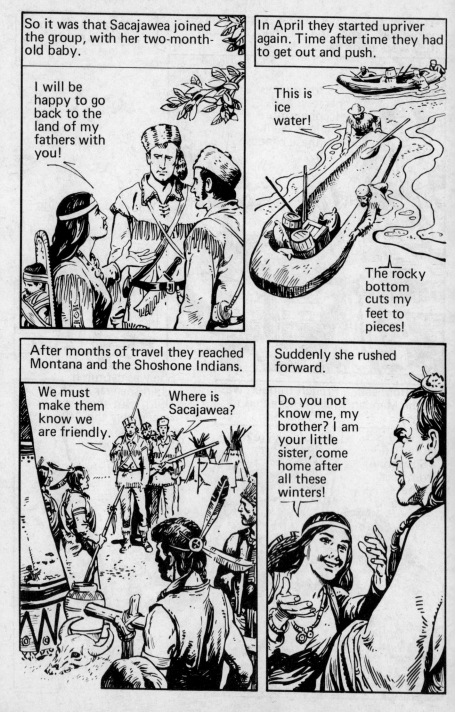

Hunger was what hurt the most. There was little game among the bare rocks.

Did you shoot anything?

Not much to feed all our hungry people!

At last, on September 19 they dragged themselves into a Nez Perce* village looking like scarecrows.

Pray God God they're friendly!

We can't—look like much danger to them!

Tired, hungry, ill, they could not yet know what they had done. They had crossed the Rockies. They were near the headwaters of the Columbia River, on the last part of their journey. The Indians took them in, fed and cared for them.

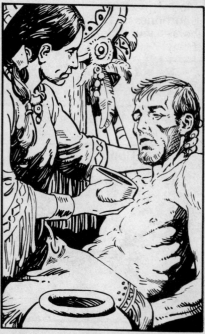

* a tribe of Indians who lived in the northwest

Soon they were strong enough to build new canoes. They were ready to sail the swiftly-flowing streams and rivers that would carry them, they hoped, to the Pacific Ocean.

Often they were in dangerous waters.

Many times they had to travel on foot around water that flowed too fast.

November 7 was a day of pouring rain and fog. But suddenly the fog rolled away.

Look! The Pacific Ocean!

We have reached the mouth of the Columbia River and the western edge of our country!

They built another fort and settled in. They named it Fort Clatsop for the nearby Indians.

If a ship arrives, at least some of us can return by sea.

The Indians have been asked to let us know if one stops anywhere along this coast.

They spent long hours boiling salt out of sea water.

We'll keep hunters out every day. Then we can preserve the extra meat with sea salt.

The cold, rainy winter passed.

It is March again, but no ships!

It's time to start back the way we came!

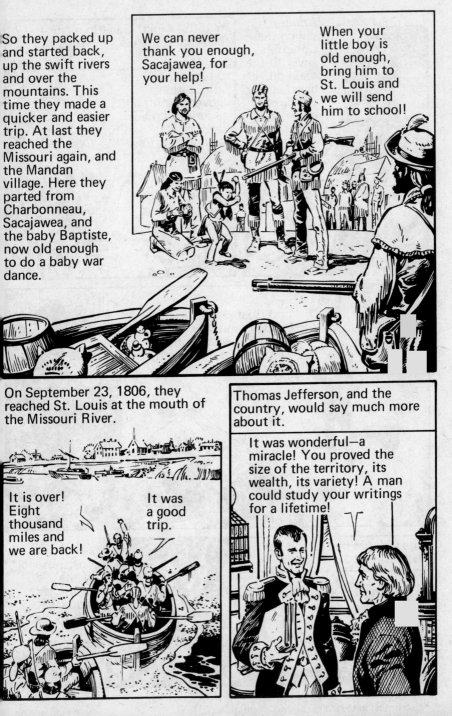

So they packed up and started back, up the swift rivers and over the mountains. This time they made a quicker and easier trip. At last they reached the Missouri again, and the Mandan village. Here they parted from Charbonneau, Sacajawea, and the baby Baptiste, now old enough to do a baby war dance.

We can never thank you enough, Sacajawea, for your help!

When your little boy is old enough, bring him to St. Louis and we will send him to school!

On September 23, 1806, they reached St. Louis at the mouth of the Missouri River.

It is over! Eight thousand miles and we are back!

It was a good trip.

Thomas Jefferson, and the country, would say much more about it.

It was wonderful—a miracle! You proved the size of the territory, its wealth, its variety! A man could study your writings for a lifetime!

And by sailing the Columbia River to the sea, you've given us our strongest claim on Oregon!

In 1808, Albert Gallatin made a report to Congress.

I recommend that the National government build a series of roads and canals connecting East and West.

Congress acted.

I ask that we put aside enough money to build a national road from Cumberland, Maryland, to St. Louis, Missouri.

The bill was passed and came to President Jefferson.

Will you sign it or veto* it?

Is it constitutional** for the government to do such work? I don't think so.

* refuse to let a bill become a law
** according to the United States Constitution

Building was begun, using a new process invented by a Scot named McAdam.

It's called a "macadamized" road. The more it is used, the better it gets!

But think what such a road would mean for settling the West! I'll sign it!

The National or Cumberland Road, today U.S. 40, was a success. Horses and wagons could travel at ten miles an hour. It was much better than any other road we had, and added greatly to the flow of western travel.

This used to be a quiet country road.

It seems as if everybody in the world is moving West.

On August 9, 1807, people along the Hudson River in New York watched a great event.

When will it get here, Father?

Maybe never, son! Some call it "Fulton's Folly."

Tell me about it again. I can't understand how it works.

It's a boat with a steam engine on it. The engine turns a paddle wheel, and that makes the boat move.

Look! Something's coming!

Look at it go!

Wonderful! No sails, no oars! It's a new age beginning!

Robert Fulton's *Clermont,* going five miles an hour, sailed from New York to Albany in thirty-two hours.

DeWitt Clinton, governor of New York, was quick to see its good points.

These steamboats will completely change river travel!

Yes?

They can carry goods up and down the Ohio and Mississippi, between Lake Erie and New Orleans. They can sail between the port of New York and Albany . . .

So?

With a waterway across the state joining us with the West, New York could bcome the greatest port in the country!

In 1817, New York agreed to the building of a canal* 363 miles long. Not everyone liked it.

What are they building?

That's Clinton's ditch. Fool idea! It's supposed to connect the Hudson River with Lake Erie.

* a waterway built for travel

It took eight years to finish the Erie Canal. On October 26, 1826, a large number of canal boats started from Buffalo.

In every village the mules were frightened by cheering crowds.

Hurrah! Three cheers for the Erie Canal! Hurrah for Clinton's ditch!

The lead boat carried two barrels of water from Lake Erie to New York. Clinton poured the lake water into the sea as cannons fired a salute.

The canal was a great success. At once the cost of sending goods dropped $100 a ton to $8. It made New York a great city, and carried thousands of passengers west.

The first railroad in the United States was very small. It opened in Quincy, Massachusetts in 1826.

They've found horses can haul a much heavier load on rails than on a road.

That's wonderful!

Then someone figured out how to put a steam engine in a locomotive.

One thing is certain—railroads are the travel of the future!

Sort of an "iron horse"?

In 1828, the Baltimore and Ohio Railroad Company started building tracks. It was slow work.

In 1830, the Baltimore and Ohio put its first small locomotive* into service. It was called *Tom Thumb*.

How long has this been going on?

Two years! And they've built only fourteen miles of track.

By 1850 there would be 9,000 miles of track connecting the major cities of the East. It would carry goods and people between East and West.

* train engine

St. Louis, on the frontier*, was the "gateway to the West." Lewis and Clark started and ended their trip there. In 1819, William Ashley of Missouri went into a St. Louis newspaper office.

It would become the Ashley Rocky Mountain Company. And among the men Ashley talked to were names that would change the future of the West. One of them was Jim Beckwourth.

* a border land between wild and lived-in places

Jed Smith, Jim Bridger, Bill Sublette, Tom Fitzpatrick—these were other men who would try it. Some worked for companies, some alone. In their love of the forests and their search for valuable furs, they would explore the far west to the Pacific. They would find the passes through the mountains and open the way for the settlers who would follow. They were the mountain men.

By mid-September they reached their first stop, the Pawnee camp at Ottumwa.

*dried meat mixed with spices and berries

In the morning, Jim Beckwourth watched the Indians prepare.

They ride the work-horses to keep their ponies fresh for the charge.

The dogs will pull the empty travoises* to the hunt. Then the workhorses will pull the loaded travoises back to the village.

Come, we will watch the hunt from Tekiha Ridge.

Like an army, the mounted braves, yelping dogs and squaws** moved across the grassy plain.

* a type of stretcher made of hides attached to poles

** Indian women

For two hours the crowd moved north. Then two scouts appeared.

The herd is two leagues north, on the Oahe Plains. A large one!

We can drive them between the hills.

Is there danger of driving them over the cliffs?

No, we will kill all we need before the buffalo reach the cliffs.

Take your braves and circle the herd from the hills.

Bands of hunters, now on their fastest ponies, moved quietly toward the nearby hills.

From Tekhia Ridge, Jim saw his first large buffalo herd. They covered the plain like a gray blanket, still in the noonday heat. All was quiet; no Indians were in sight.

Chief Two-Axe looked around him. He held up a spear.

He threw the spear high into the sky. There was a great cry.

AIEEEee-ee-ee!

Even before the spear curved downward, the hills exploded with Indians. The braves rode toward the buffalo from three sides, with screeching cries and galloping hoofs. The buffalo ran off. The hunt had begun!

Holding his spear with one hand and his pony's mane with the other, each brave rode into the herd of buffalo.

Choosing one animal each, the hunters drove their spears into the necks of the buffalo.

AII-EE-eeeeeeeeeeee!

The attack moved on, leaving dozens of dead animals on the plain.

Don't they ever miss?

No, they are proud of their skill at always hitting the right spot.

Finally Two-Axe gave new orders.

Call off the hunt! And send the braves to turn the herd away from the cliffs!

Won't it be dangerous—turning that herd?

Braves might be hurt, but we cannot let buffalo kill themselves rushing over cliffs! Next spring, Pawnees will need buffalo again.

Now Jim saw the plain turned into a regular factory.

They must take care of the meat before it spoils. The braves will skin the buffalo and cut up the meat.

The next morning the squaws pounded the dried meat into powder and mixed it with spices and berries. Then they coated it with melted buffalo fat, and packed it into buffalo skin cases.

Next day the group left the Indian village.

So that's pemmican! How does it taste?

Next winter when game is scarce, you'll think it tastes fine.

Goodbye, Two-Axe. See you next spring!

Good hunting!

At Fort Clark, Ashley divided the party into six groups, each with a different territory.

All right, men. We'll meet back here on April 1. Good luck!

Jim went with Ashley, Fitzpatrick, Lajeunesse, and a Pawnee guide. They rode into the eastern Rockies.

How far have we come?

Maybe 300 miles.

Suddenly from behind there was a scuffling sound.

She slipped! She was carrying our food!

Quickly the mule was swept away.

All our food was on that mule!

We're at least a week from Fort Clark.

We can't make it without food. We must hunt.

They camped that night without food. In the morning, snow was in the air.

All right, men, let's go.

To find game, you must go beyond forest.

The Indian will stay here to guard the animals. The rest of us will go off in four directions.

If you kill anything, fire two shots. We'll come back here. If it's something big, we'll all go to carry it in.

Jim started in the direction Ashley told him.

He walked for hours, stopping only to mark his way.

He felt a shaking under him. He put his ear to the ground.

Antelope!* I'm sure of it!

* an animal like a deer

And it'll take all of us to carry back the meat! Now come and eat.

Enough meat for two weeks! We're saved!

Well supplied with meat, Lajeunesse was able to make the trip back to Fort Clark for more food. Meanwhile, the others went on to the winter camp.

Good winter camp here!

We'll get our cabin built and our traps out.

In spite of the snow and cold, the winter passed quickly. Every day there was work to do.

The traps must be set and the catch removed . . .

But a roaring fire kept the cabin warm.

The trapped beavers were skinned and the skins dressed.

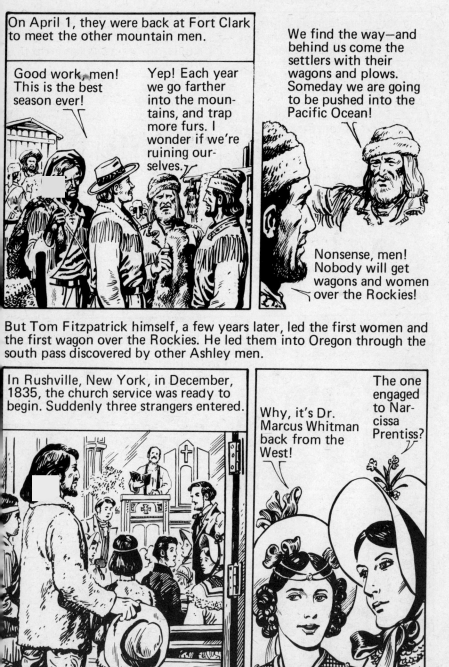

On April 1, they were back at Fort Clark to meet the other mountain men.

Good work, men! This is the best season ever!

Yep! Each year we go farther into the mountains, and trap more furs. I wonder if we're ruining ourselves.

We find the way—and behind us come the settlers with their wagons and plows. Someday we are going to be pushed into the Pacific Ocean!

Nonsense, men! Nobody will get wagons and women over the Rockies!

But Tom Fitzpatrick himself, a few years later, led the first women and the first wagon over the Rockies. He led them into Oregon through the south pass discovered by other Ashley men.

In Rushville, New York, in December, 1835, the church service was ready to begin. Suddenly three strangers entered.

Why, it's Dr. Marcus Whitman back from the West!

The one engaged to Narcissa Prentiss?

Not only were Marcus Whitman and Narcissa deeply in love, but they shared the same goals.

It is true! The Indians beyond the Rockies are calling for the gospel. The church will send us together to teach them!

We will do God's work together!

They were married, and on March 3, 1836 they left homes and families to begin the long trip to Oregon.

God keep you till we meet again!

Goodbye! Goodbye!

They went by steamboat to Cincinnati, to St. Louis, to Liberty, Missouri, the end of the line. With them went the two Indian boys, and two other missionaries,* Eliza and Henry Spalding.

The company boat will pick us up here and take us on to Council Bluffs, where we'll meet the fur caravan.

After ten days' wait, they heard the company steamer in the river.

Stop! Wait!

Sorry—no room for more passengers!

* people who brought the Christian faith to the Indians

There was only one thing to do. Whitman bought riding horses and a wagon for luggage. Then they started off across the plains.

There were dangerous rivers to cross.

Don't worry, Marcus! We'll make it!

After days of hard riding, they met the first challenge and caught up with the fur trappers. Its leader was Tom Fitzpatrick.

You've given us the honor, ma'am, of being the first group ever to take white women over the mountains!

Through the heat and dust the trappers followed the River Platte.

They say the Platte is a thousand miles long and six inches deep!

On the treeless plain, Narcissa and Eliza learned to make fires out of dried buffalo droppings.

Fresh buffalo meat every day! What a luxury!

I don't think it agrees with me.

After two months they were riding through the south pass, the gateway to Oregon. Just ahead was the fur trappers' meeting place.

What happens at the meeting place, Tom?

Why, ma'am, the trappers get together and enjoy themselves after a hard winter.

They'll sell their furs . . . eat and drink and play cards. Some of them will spend in a few days the money they've worked all winter to make!

More important to the Whitmans, the meeting place was the end of the trail for the fur trappers.

I've met two English fur traders from the Hudson's Bay Company. Perhaps they'll let us go on to Oregon with them.

The Englishmen, McLeod and McKay, talked the matter over.

We don't want American trappers in Oregon—or American settlers!

But missionaries to the Indians are a different matter. Why not give them our help?

McLeod did not know that he was taking a big step toward losing Oregon for his country.

They set out with the English party. Six weeks' travel over the roughest part of the trail lay ahead.

They call these the Blue Mountains.

They're very beautiful—and very steep!

The last part of the journey was down the Columbia River.

What a wonderful ride!

At Fort Vancouver, they were greeted by the British agent, Dr. McLoughlin.

Why are all the flags flying? Is it a holiday?

Ah, madame, we are honoring the first white women ever to sail down the Columbia!

The Whitmans started a mission* among the Cayuse Indians at a spot called Waiilatpu.

I will soon build furniture, and add more rooms.

Our parents must have made a similar start in western New York!

The Sunday services the Whitmans held were well attended by the Indians.

The children came daily to Narcissa's school classes.

Indian sign here —English word here!

RIVERS
BIRDS
BUFFALO
MOON

* a program of lessons in religion and school work

Whitman was delighted by the rich soil.

I am going to plant wheat and corn. And I'll build a mill!

I'd like to see this land filled with neat farms and happy families—American families!

The Whitmans and others sent word back East of the wonders of Oregon. In September, 1842, a band of settlers just over the mountains arrived.

Welcome to Waiilatpu!

I am pleased to see white folks and houses! We had to leave the wagons at Snake Fort, but 112 of us made it with horses and pack mules!

But Marcus had decided. He would save the mission—and he would do more! He would go to Washington and see the president. There he would show Congress that this was the time to claim Oregon for the United States!

In May, 1843, a great wagon train gathered at Independence, Missouri. It was ready to roll west with 2,000 animals, 1,000 people, and 100 wagons. They kept turning to one man for advice—Marcus Whitman.

Travel, travel, travel! Nothing else will take you to the end of your journey! Nothing is good that causes a moment's delay!

When there were rivers to cross, he rode first, finding a firm bottom.

They passed the great plains sights.

Scott's Bluff . . .

Chimney Rock . . .

Independence Rock, where the men carved their names.

At Fort Hall in September, they were told by a British officer to leave their wagons there.

You cannot take wagons through! You'll be lucky to make it with horses without starving to death!

Marcus did not agree.

Keep your wagons and animals! You'll need them for farming. If we pull together, we can haul the wagons through in spite of everything!

Take the wagons! On to Oregon! Oregon for the Americans!

The Snake River was the worst river yet. It was fast, wide, and deep. They chained the wagons together.

Now, all together-r-r-r-r!

Men went ahead to make the mountain trails passable.

If there was no other way, they lifted the wagons over.

But they made it. A thousand settlers, 100 wagons, had come over the Oregon trail safely. Many more would follow.

God's angels watched over you and brought you home!

In spring, 1846, the people who came over the Rockies brought news.

The treaty is ended! Britain and the United States won't share the territory any longer!

But which will Oregon be— British or American?

Don't know! It was not settled when we left. There could be war . . .

In the Columbia River at Oregon City, two warships waited: the British *Modeste,* and the American *Shark.*

In late winter of 1847, a ship arrived from Hawaii carrying Honolulu newspapers.

Any news?

News . . . NEWS?

A treaty was signed with England last June! All land south of the forty-ninth parallel* is American!

In Oregon City, the people went wild with excitement. The American flag was raised. Cannons fired from the *Shark*.

It's settled! We're Americans! Right through to the Pacific Ocean!

* an imaginary line around the earth which measures distance from the equator

Words to know

1. antelope
2. canal
3. constitutional
4. frontier
5. locomotive
6. mission

7. missionaries
8. Nez Perce
9. parallel
10. pemmican
11. squaw
12. veto

Questions

1. Why did President Jefferson want to buy New Orleans from the French?

2. What made France offer to sell the whole Louisiana Territory to the U.S.?

3. Why were Lewis and Clark sent to explore the Louisiana Territory?

4. Name some of the Indian tribes who lived in the central and western parts of the country. Were they friendly or unfriendly?

5. How did the Indian woman Sacajawea help Lewis and Clark?

6. What were some of the inventions and discoveries that made trade and travel easier during the early 1800s?

7. Why were the missionaries of this time so eager to travel into the West?

8. What were some of the methods of travel used to reach the West?

9. What territory won from England first extended the United States from the Atlantic to the Pacific?

10. What animal did the plains Indians make great use of for food, shelter, and clothing?

Match the following people and objects with the things they are famous for:

1.	*Clermont*	a.	name of first locomotive
2.	railroad locomotive	b.	name of first steamboat
3.	Mr. McAdam	c.	invented the steamboat
4.	De Witt Clinton	d.	sold Louisiana Territory to the U.S.
5.	Columbia		
6.	Livingston and Monroe	e.	explored the Louisiana Territory
7.	Robert Fulton		
8.	*Tom Thumb*	f.	arranged to build the Erie Canal
9.	Talleyrand		
10.	Lewis and Clark	g.	nicknamed the "iron horse"
		h.	bought Louisiana Territory from France
		i.	invented a new type of road
		j.	river which flows into the Pacific Ocean

Complete the following sentences

1. Besides the explorers and missionaries, ＿＿＿＿＿＿＿＿ helped to open up trails to the West for settlers.

2. The city known as the "gateway to the West" is＿＿＿＿＿.

3. Two crops which grew very well in the midwest and in the northwest were＿＿＿＿＿ and＿＿＿＿＿.

4. The Erie Canal connected Lake Erie with＿＿＿＿＿.

5. The Americans learned a great deal about their new country from the＿＿＿＿＿.